A CHURCH ON BROADWAY

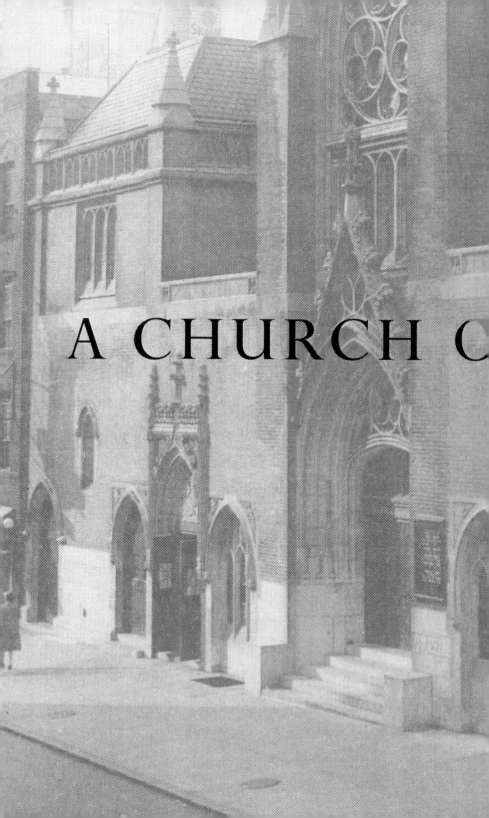

A CHURCH C

N BROADWAY

The Story

of

St. Malachy's

The Actors' Chapel

A CHURCH ON BROADWAY:
THE STORY OF ST. MALACHY'S, THE ACTORS' CHAPEL

Published
September 2006
by
St. Malachy's Church
239 West 49th Street
New York, NY 10019

ISBN: 1-4243-1054-7

Printed in the United States of America

10 9 8 7 6 5 4 3 2 1

Jonathan F. Englert, *editor/writer*
Kathleen Baldonado, *production editor*
Glen Edelstein, *designer*
Rudi Papiri, *writer and photographer*
Mary Brendle, *district historian*
Jess Espinoza, *interviewer/writer*
Carlass Pond, *interviewer/writer*
José Fermin, *interviewer/writer*
Andy Hoets, *photographer*
Olivier Imbert, *designer*
Penelope Thomas, *designer/photographer*

Also special thanks to Father Richard D. Baker,
Father Joseph A. Kelly, Sister Elizabeth Hasselt, O.P.,
Sister Lillian McNamara, O.P.,
Monsignor Michael C. Crimmins,
Stephanie Budelman, Joy Pascua-Kim, Peggy Pugh,
Maryann Chach and everyone at the
Shubert Archives.

Dear artists, you well know that there are many impulses which, either from within or from without, can inspire your talent. Every genuine inspiration, however, contains some tremor of that "breath" with which the Creator Spirit suffused the work of creation from the very beginning. Overseeing the mysterious laws governing the universe, the divine breath of the Creator Spirit reaches out to human genius and stirs its creative power. He brings together the sense of the good and the beautiful, and he awakens energies of mind and heart, which enable it to conceive an idea and give it form in a work of art. It is right then to speak, even if only analogically, of "moments of grace," because the human being is able to experience in some way the Absolute who is utterly beyond.

—*from* The Way of Beauty, Letter of His Holiness Pope John Paul II to Artists *(April 4, 1999)*

A CHURCH ON BROADWAY

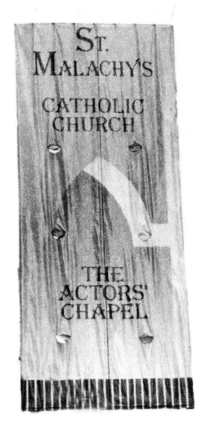

WE PRESENT THIS book as a "little gem" for all, and as such an apt tribute to the "little gem" on Broadway, St. Malachy's, the Actors' Chapel—the extraordinary church that inspired these pages. Here you will find a history and diverse reflections on this place. But, even more important, you will find a living spirit. The spirit will be recognizable for all those who have even briefly encountered St. Malachy's. Proceed with caution: This spirit is infectious, and once bitten, a lifelong attachment to St. Malachy's usually follows.

Father Richard Baker, pastor of St. Malachy's.

To begin to explore why this is, let me offer the following insights of Father Thomas A. Lynch, a brother priest and colleague at St. Joseph's Seminary, delivered on the occasion of my installation as pastor on March 21, 2004:

St. Malachy's occupies a unique place in the history of New York. The church is, to quote Cardinal Patrick Hayes, "a temple of God in the greatest playground in the world!"

I couldn't help but enjoy the published account of when the first mass was celebrated in St. Malachy's over one hundred years ago. The Catholic News announced that the new chapel of St. Malachy's on West 49th Street opened for services on Thursday evening, October 29, 1903. Furthermore, the Catholic News reported that it was probably the first time in the history of the Catholic Church in New York that a church was dedicated at night. How ironic when you think about it. About thirty years later, the pastors of St. Malachy's sought and received what was then a very unusual permission from the archbishop to cele-

brate mass at midnight and at 4 A.M., to accommodate the hundreds of people in the entertainment industry, from the dishwasher to the waiter and waitress to the showgirl to the actor and actress.

The Catholic News went on to report that a mass had been celebrated on the Sunday before the Thursday evening dedication. On that day, the new congregation of St. Malachy's was temporarily attending mass in a hall while the church was being cleaned and renovated. However, on this particular Sunday, churchgoers were unable to gain admittance into the hall because—and this really is in print—the janitor who usually opened the door was fast asleep, and they were unable to wake him to come and unlock the door from the inside. So they and their new pastor, Father William Daly, marched down to the new chapel, walked around the scaffolding, cleared away a few drop cloths, moved a bunch of brooms, dusted off a few chairs and celebrated their first mass in this church. Right from the beginning of St. Malachy's history, there is a record of adjustment on behalf of her people. Right from the beginning of St. Malachy's history, there is a determination to stay awake even when others sleep.

This book is a record and a celebration of St. Malachy's first century, with its many pastors and parishioners. It is filled with celebrities and noncelebrities, all of whom share an important bond: their fondness for this particular church. But this book is also a forward-looking statement, because St. Malachy's continues its mission of reaching out . . . of staying awake even when others sleep. Today, not unlike yesterday, St. Malachy's does this by inspiring and being inspired by the energy, talent and diversity of the community that surrounds it. A glance at the website (www.actorschapel.org) or the weekly bulletin will reveal a living community: a superb choir, theatrical performances, art exhibitions, senior and community outreach—it's all happening here, and it's growing.

I hope you enjoy this book both as a history and a tribute, but also perhaps as an invitation to visit the church yourself someday, and join the many who have passed through its doors and experienced this profound sanctuary on the Great White Way.

 ST. MALACHY HAD always wanted to live in France. . . . instead he just died there. But saints are saints because they don't do what they want to do. They go where there is need. They do the work that requires doing. They submit to divine will. They keep their vows. And most of all, they never seem to consider any of this extraordinary.

It's said that when you are looking at a saint, you are not looking at an amazing human being so much as you are looking at a human being the way a human being was meant to be. They are cleansed of those impediments that prevent us from assuming our rightful place in the world by prayer, self-sacrifice and grace. To meet a saint, then, is to meet someone who is exactly who he or she is supposed to be at that moment. As far as the record shows, St. Malachy, or Maolmhaodag Ua Morgair, was just such a human being.

The Ireland into which St. Malachy was born in 1094 had been Christian for six hundred years, but the quality of its Christianity was questionable. Many had lapsed, paganism was on the ascent, vicious politicking was the rule. . . . Ireland needed a reformer.

Malachy would spend his life as that reformer. He was devoted but reluctant because he was a man of strong monastic inclinations who found himself mired in a public life. He spent many years restoring what had been lost: the divine office and the use of the sacraments of confession, confirmation and marriage. He brought wayward kings back to the faith, and by his early thirties had become a bishop—a bishop who would take to the streets to preach until his people came into the churches. He slipped away to a monastery for a time, but was forced to re-emerge to save Ireland again as the archbishop of Armagh.

Malachy never managed to settle into the monastic life for which he yearned. However, during a trip to Rome, he visited St. Bernard of Clairvaux and the Cistercians, and found a place well-suited to his contemplative tastes. He asked the Pope for permission to remain, but permission was denied and Malachy returned to ten more years of public life in Ireland, which he dispatched with vigor.

After that decade, he ventured to Rome a second time, but he never arrived. He stopped at Clairvaux to see Bernard, but after celebrating mass with his friend, he developed a high fever. Malachy died at the monastery with Bernard beside him on November 2, 1148, the Feast of All Souls.

THE ACTORS' CHAPEL

A LITTLE MORE than fifty years ago, E. B. White, author of *Charlotte's Web* and *Stuart Little*, penned a short essay entitled "Here is New York." Wisely, the piece did not attempt to relate a definitive history of this great city. Instead, it ventured to capture New York's spirit—and this it did (and then some) even though by this time White was permanently installed on his New England farm. Judging from the freshness and relevance of his work today, it is clear that something essential in the spirit of the city has remained unchanged down through the years.

Today, St. Malachy's is dwarfed by residential high-rises built over the last decade.

Such is the case with St. Malachy's, a church that is both an integral part of this city and also a world unto itself. This is a place where time stands still and also a place where time's joyous and melancholy passage is recorded. It is a marker that has measured many kinds of tides over a century. There has been the ever-rising tide of construction, as buildings many times the church's height have grown up around it and eclipsed its spires. The fluctuating tide of the neighborhood's fortunes from birth to decline to renewal and rebirth. And then there is the tide of people, both the committed parishioners and the stray visitors, the famous and the anonymous, who have flowed in and out the door for these one hundred years (so many people—and so varied—that this book has little hope of doing them justice).

But most of all it is a sacred place. It is a place where at least twice daily the sacrifice of the mass nourishes (and also occasionally rebukes) the world around the church. A place out of which flows the countless unheralded sacrifices of the many people who find solace and strength here, and bring themselves out into the world beyond its doors. This place has been a constant in the hubbub and change of the Great White Way, the rare marquee with a permanent star, but also a subject of

13

change, makeover and reinvention. Cardinal Hayes, offi-
ciating at the dedication of an expanded church in 1930,
had this to say:

> *It is a glorious thing to realize that this tabernacle
> of Christ is set up here in one of the greatest play-
> grounds of the world. . . .This church is the center
> of a world of make-believe, a world of unreality. . . .
> But there is nothing make-believe or unreal about
> this church.*

To enter into this place is to experience sanctuary
and its quiet, assured reality. But linger for a moment
more with E. B. White:

> *The city is like poetry: it compresses life, all races
> and breeds, into a small island and adds music and
> the accompaniment of internal engines. The island
> of Manhattan is without any doubt the greatest
> human concentrate on earth, the poem whose
> magic is comprehensible to millions of permanent
> residents but whose full meaning will always
> remain elusive.*

"I have been living on Eighth Avenue for twenty-five years and I have been coming to St. Malachy's all that time. I just became attached to it. I always think of St. Malachy's as my home."

—*Prima Stephen*, parishioner

Each person encounters the city in his or her own way, and to the music of his or her own poetry. So, too, does one encounter St. Malachy's. The stories of its visitors are the stories of individuals, celebrities and not, who have encountered St. Malachy's and are the better for it. They are human stories, historical stories and, fundamentally, spiritual stories. At St. Malachy's, the theater is never very far away, and so we find Antonio Banderas entering this silent space as a relative unknown almost two decades ago and uttering an enthusiastic, youthful prayer inspired by his first visit to Broadway: "Jesus, I would love to work in this place someday." Or Anny EmTaylor, a beloved longtime parishioner, whose arrival at St. Malachy's and conversion to Catholicism were at least partly inspired by Bing Crosby's *Going My Way*, which was shot here in 1944. Banderas happened upon St. Malachy's and the peace of its sanctuary; the silver screen drew EmTaylor. But both encountered a space that had a shared, communal history (one they both became a part of) and also a profoundly unique history that began with them.

There is a photograph that I encountered in writing this book, the image of which has returned to mind several times since I first saw it in the church's archives. A man, bearing a faint resemblance to an English Bobby,

A street cleaner and surroundings (circa 1900) provide a sense of neighborhood two years before construction began for St. Malachy's.

sweeps a cobblestone street with a stiff broom. He is some kind of sanitation worker, appears very official and seems to be doing his work with profound seriousness. In the background, are a horse and carriage and the Victorian awnings on a nearby building. The paper of the photograph is browning. The location and the year are noted: "48th Street and 8th Avenue, 1900." This scene, then, occurred less than two years before ground was broken for St. Malachy's only one block down and a third of a crosstown block east. Perhaps it is an imaginative conspiracy of broom (and its suggestion of a clean sweep) and the reams of historical information and personal biography that I have absorbed in preparing to write this essay, but the image overwhelms me with the sheer magnitude of life and effort that has played out around and within St. Malachy's over a century.

There is a difference between a mystery and a question mark. Some places are the latter: curiosities until their questions are puzzled out, and then no longer capable of holding sway. But St. Malachy's is a mystery. It is a mystery that this little church, with its stout Gothic soul and Byzantine eccentricities, was set afloat on a tide of restless demographics and has survived a century. It experienced decline and then the appearance of a

17

In some ways, the arc of composer **Paul Creston's** *life parallels the history of St. Malachy's in the twentieth century: an early struggle against the odds, a rapid, well-earned rise, a dark period in the wilderness and a later resurgence.*

Paul Creston was born in New York City in 1906. The son of a Sicilian housepainter, he was christened Giuseppe Guttoveggio. His musical talent became evident at an early age and his parents supported it as best they could with limited means. By his early teens he had surpassed the ability of his piano teacher and seemed well on his way to realizing his musical potential as both a performer and a composer. But lack of money forced him to abandon high school after only two years in order to earn money for his family as an errand boy, bank clerk and, later, an insurance claim examiner.

Creston once declared: "I make no special effort to be American. I conscientiously work to be my true self, which is Italian by parentage, American by birth, and cosmopolitan by choice."

But his story of self-reliance and tireless devotion to his music suggests a very American story indeed. He changed his name and began a rigorous course of self-study aimed at developing both his music and his general knowledge. He reasoned that if Thomas Edison could get by on four hours' sleep a night, he could too. And he was known to smoke ground coffee beans late into the night to stay awake as he read the classics of literature, philosophy and history—only after he had spent several hours practicing his music and composing. Thus, he maintained a veritable self-guided conservatory.

His first musical employment came in 1926 when he played the organ for silent movies. When the talkies came in, he was out of work, but was soon hired as the organist

for St. Malachy's Church. St. Malachy's would provide a stable platform for his composition work for the next thirty-three years.

It was during this period that Paul Creston distinguished himself as one of the foremost American composers of his time, a man who at his height rivaled Copland for the title of Composer Most Played in American Concert Halls.

Creston's break came in 1933 when he approached the composer Henry Cowell with his "Seven Theses" for piano. Soon commissions and other honors came. He was awarded two Guggenheim Fellowships (in 1938 and 1939) and the New York Music Critics Circle Award for his first symphony, among a host of other major awards. He taught composition and piano, and in addition to his formal composition work, wrote many scores for television and radio, winning an Emmy for his score to the documentary In the American Grain (1964). Throughout the 1950s, Creston's creativity and popularity grew rapidly. He became well-known internationally and his music was played in programs with Gershwin, Barber and Harris, and by conductors like Arturo Toscanini, Leopold Stokowski and Eugene Ormandy.

But by the 1960s his music had fallen out of favor as attention turned toward more experimental works. Creston continued to compose at a blistering pace. He died in Poway, California, on August 24, 1985, just as the first hints of a renewal of interest in his work occurred.

This renewal continues today. As Gerard Schwartz, conductor of the Seattle Symphony, recalled when discussing a new recording of Creston's powerful "Symphony No. 3": "If he had lived long enough . . . he would have been reaping the great success he deserved due to his kind of music being back in favor and accepted for what it is: part of the great American symphonic tradition."

The upper church with pews perpendicular to altar as they were for the greater part of the twentieth century.

charismatic and driven priest who ushered in a renewal that became one of its finest hours. Not just once . . . but twice. Not only did it survive; it flourished.

But these mysteries stem from the central mystery of this church itself. While it is true that community churches tend to fire loyalty and commitment in their parishioners, the spirit found among those drawn to St.

Malachy's is different. Not simply to be dismissed as the dramatic tendency of "those theater people," the spirit of its devotees is more vigorous than would be explained by the usual parish conditions (e.g., the site of a baptism, a wedding or a funeral). St. Malachy's is seen as a home, a benefactor, even as a Broadway personality, and far too dear to ever imagine losing. In these pages, Edward Hermann comments that New York would not be New York without St. Malachy's. What does this mean exactly? Checkered cabs; the Five Points; the Elevated (the train that ran aboveground before being replaced with the current subway line)—for some, these might have been New York. These, though, have all been swept away. But if the word went out tomorrow that the bulldozers were coming for St. Malachy's demolition, I wouldn't be the least surprised if a raffle would have to be held to choose who, among a throng of volunteers, would chain themselves to its front doors. Today, I would hope to win that raffle, though ten years ago, before I encountered this church, I would have been indifferent. Why does St. Malachy's evoke such commitment in people?

To some extent, this must remain a mystery. But I think part of the answer lies at that juncture where the intensely personal and internal meets the historical, the external and the urban. And it also lies in the fact that people are committed to St. Malachy's because St. Malachy's has been committed to them. Classical religious art often depicts a church being held in the giant palm of its patron saint. The church appears as a tiny thing—the mere model of a church—and the saint looms like a collosus, benevolently holding their namesake high above the world and utterly secure. The iconic Malachy of this Broadway church would be different— less above the earth, more firmly upon it. Not a distant and visibly powerful figure as much as a fervent, understanding, compassionate and enormously likable one. Someone good at parties and also at the soberest, most reverential moments. He would be depicted venturing forth from his church and returning with inspired men and women, who together would help lift the church high and hold it secure.

SOME CHURCHES BEGIN as a *fait accompli*, seemingly guaranteed that there will always be a community to serve. St. Malachy's might have begun life like that, when the great population boom of turn-of-the-century New York seemed to assure the new parish of a flock. But then

St. Malachy's before reconstruction in the 1920s brought its front steps inside the church.

this flock disappeared. Thus began an outward-seeking life that continues today and is found in these inspired men and women and the pastors who have led them.

When I first learned of St. Malachy's, I wasn't yet Catholic and I wasn't living in New York. That would happen several years later. I learned about the church through my cousin, an actor and writer, who attended mass there and visited seniors through Encore. St. Malachy's existed at the fringes of my conception of New York just as my religious faith, what little there was of a confusing and non-binding array of sentiment and theology, existed at the fringes of my life. It was a mere suggestion of something, but a beguiling suggestion. A facade somewhere with a doorway that beckoned.

If New York has an existential mission, it must be to make both the city's visitors and its inhabitants terribly aware of impermanence and transition. If the changing skyline doesn't do it, the sidewalk rush of faces will. A New Yorker will revisit a familiar neighborhood five years after moving to another part of town and be astounded by how many shops have closed and how many have opened. The theater district does it with changing marquees. The longest shows—no matter how well-loved— seldom survive into their teens.

St. Malachy's was the obvious choice for **Raymond Arroyo**, *EWTN news director and author of the bestselling* Mother Angelica: The Remarkable Story of a Nun, Her Nerve, and a Network of Miracles. *When Arroyo studied acting with Stella Adler and Uta Hagen, he was in the theater district all the time. He discovered St. Malachy's while walking down the street, and later became intrigued because of the many legendary actors who made the church part of their lives on Broadway. He, too, joined in the tradition, frequently dropping in to St. Malachy's to go to mass before a show.*

Even though I was born in Manhattan, we soon moved away and when I came back in the early 1990s, I returned to the city as an outsider. For the outsider, New York reveals itself in bits and pieces. You notice the entrance to a building. Then you notice it again a few weeks later. At some point you enter out of curiosity or, more likely, on some business. An association grows and gradually your understanding of New York, your poem, comes to include this place.

I first saw St. Malachy's, the facade, at the time of my return and connected it with my cousin's stories about it. As he told it, the place was so much larger than life, but here was a tiny church with a dingy exterior in what still felt like a borderline neighborhood. It might have been closed, but I doubt that at that time I would have gone in even if it was open. From time to time, I passed the church, always noticing it and finding something in myself being fired by its sight. But it was only after a conversion experience and my subsequent reception into the Catholic Church that I finally walked through its doors. I will never forget the day. At the time, my faith was very new, fervent but fearful, raw and in search of comfort and consolation. I say this only by way of attempting to express, through the sensibilities of one very much in need of peace, what it was that I felt crossing the threshold from the midtown street at noon, with its grating rash of noise, and finding my way to kneel before that extraordinary mosaic of Christ in the West Chapel. The church was so quiet it seemed I could hear the candles burning. The stillness of the church seemed such a miracle. At that moment, St. Malachy's assumed a permanent and indelible part of my life. I attended mass there regularly and over time became a friendly visitor in the Encore program, but these were just the fruits of this initial experience, and the fruits flowed from the mystery of this encounter. It is probably such a mystery that explains so many people's commitment to this church.

The permit that authorized the construction of a vault that extended St. Malachy's farther onto the sidewalk and covered the steps.

*   *   *

NOW FOR ST. MALACHY'S, the historical entity. The church has functioned continuously since 1902. . . . At this point, many historians might adopt a tone of unassailable authority. The information presented is fact—end of story. I am prevented from adopting this tone when faced with such things as cryptic jottings on ruled composition-book paper recording (I think) the purchase of the parcels of land upon which now sits St. Malachy's.

The paper has gone brown and brittle. It seems such an informal record, as if the deal was done on the fly. At the top are four numbers separated by hyphens: 239-241-243-245. These are lot numbers. I know this because, among other things, I have poured over a map at the Shubert Archives that dated to 1879 and revealed two distinct neighborhoods. There was the neighborhood charted by the grid system—that stroke of prescient genius given the city fathers at the turn of the nineteenth century, which consequently sliced the entire, mostly rustic, island into a functional checkerboard. This is the topography with which we are familiar: Eighth Avenue to our right and Broadway to our left as we step out onto the sidewalk in front of St. Malachy's. But in superimposed

The Grotto of Our Lady of Lourdes as it appeared for most of the past century.

tracings, dotted lines and gradients of pale brown, the map suggested another neighborhood—more a world than a neighborhood. In this version, the decades receded and 239-241-243-245 dissolved into unnumbered points on Hoppers Farm, somewhere between two crooked roads: Hoppers and Verdant Lanes. The area was called Bloomingdale then, and Bloomingdale Road ran north to south through it. Later, Bloomingdale Road was widened and paved and renamed Broadway (an extension of the lower Manhattan avenue of the same name). By this time, the city was moving northward, farms seemed to have yielded to single-family homes and single-family homes to apartment buildings. A sense of the neighborhood at the time of St. Malachy's birth is elusive: Some sources refer to the comfortable country living and almost suburban tranquility of its inhabitants, others report that the district was known as the "Thieves' Lair" and overrun with tenements.

St. Malachy's appears to have been built because the Sacred Heart Church a few blocks north and to the west had a surplus of parishioners. An early report on its ministry stated that St. Malachy's cared for 2800 souls. What seems certain is that the Actors' Chapel, as St. Malachy's is often imprecisely known (imprecisely, because the

Three men crossing a hectic Times Square at the beginning of the twentieth century.

October 21st '93

ST. MALACHY'S CATHOLIC CHURCH
THE ACTORS' CHAPEL

239 West 49th Street / New York, New York 10019 / (212) 489-1340

Dear Father Kelly —
Thank you so much for your
letter — I'm sorry I can't be
with you on November 6th — I
have a performance but will
hope to join you on the 7th
On the back of this card
are a few words to be read if
you would like. Best Wishes Lynn Redgrave

Dear St Malachy's —
All of us actors can rejoice in
your rededication.
Our work requires us to
rededicate ourselves again
& again through the years.
A visit to St Malachy's
has often given me the
strength to do just that —
with love Lynn Redgrave

Actors' Chapel was in fact an actual chapel in the basement of the church), did not assume its theatrical mission immediately. On April 21, 1902, the day—if the cryptic jottings are to be believed—Lottee Acker sold lots 239 and 241 to Father Thomas P. McLaughlin for the sum of $40,000, who in turn transferred same, as well as Howard O. Leute's lot 245 (purchase price $19,500), to St. Malachy's Church for one dollar—there was no theater district to speak of. It was just getting started. Seven years earlier, Oscar Hammerstein, a plasterer, inventor, composer and impresario, had built the Olympia, the first theater in what would later become known as the theater district. His massive Olympia closed two years after its opening and drove Hammerstein into bankruptcy, but the trend had been set. In the three decades between 1900

The application for the construction of St. Malachy's, dated September 2, 1902.

and the onset of the Depression, over a hundred theaters would spring up in what was then known as the Longacre district; Longacre Square would be renamed Times Square in honor of the *New York Times;* and the "Great White Way" would become the standard coinage used to describe Broadway's marquee and billboard glow.

St. Malachy's mission emerged during this heady period. As a physical form, the church began life as a solid structure of modest proportions designed by Joseph H. McGuire and first presented to the world as Plan 541 on September 2, 1902. Plan 541, filed with the Bureau of Buildings for the Borough of Manhattan, proposed a structure that would rise a mere twelve feet from the curb to its highest point and be used as a basement church. Its foundation walls were to be built of brick, which would be erected around a base of concrete laid upon earth. Partitions would be built with brick, and studs with lath and plaster; girders would be of steel, columns of iron; floor beams would be three-by-ten-inch spruce, sixteen inches apart at their centers; brick and granite would comprise the facade.

The application is accompanied by two pieces of onion-skin typing paper. The first piece of paper rejects the application on two fine points, but the second piece notes the corrections of these points and is stamped by the Bureau. The approved roof is marked in the application as a temporary construction of tar and gravel. The flat roof would later be removed in favor of the sixty-foot-high gothic nave we know today, but for a time the adjacent rectory dwarfed the new church.

It is tempting in the absence of contrary evidence to shape the church's first twenty years into a narrative that neatly concludes in the 1920s, with St. Malachy's robust embrace of the world of the theater. Luckily, much in the record supports the temptation. The church's first two

Father Edward F. Leonard, the priest who defined St. Malachy's Broadway mission.

decades were spent as witness to a neighborhood in historic flux. Unlike the exceptionally long terms of its later pastors, the priests who served in the church's early years came and went. Thomas P. McLaughlin, known as the singing priest, barely saw the church built before he was off to New Rochelle in January 1903. His successor, William J. B. Daly, served only three years before he moved to Fordham University. Father Joseph F. Delany followed. The record goes quiet in the years between 1910 and 1920. Another building plan is filed with the city in 1910, presumably for the construction of the main body of the church as we know it today. A new architect, Thomas J. Duff, completes the form. *The walls will be coped with stone and the building heated with steam,* he writes in longhand. It is not a new building but an addition to the old, and the addition will rise sixty feet from curb to highest point (in the intervening years, interestingly, the ground beneath the foundation underwent a transformation prompting Duff to write "rock" instead of "earth" in describing what lies under St. Malachy's). Less clear is whether construction promptly followed city approval. A later source suggests the work was completed in 1917. Perhaps, but it seems unlikely. In 1910, the neighborhood that had prompted the decision to expand the church was presumably a vibrant network of families, but as the decade closed this had changed. Many sources record that later this network had shrunk as theaters came to dominate. Attendant with the theaters was an unstable churchgoing population, inhabitants of boardinghouses and hotels, characterized by hectic, usually nocturnal, schedules.

Then came Father Edward F. Leonard in 1920. This kindly-looking, avuncular figure who seemed to favor a cassock and biretta, does not strike one as a swashbuckling, theatrical type, but it is probably with him that

The ornate altar of the basement Actors' Chapel.

much of the credit for St. Malachy's Broadway reputation lies. He would serve as its pastor for more than two decades, through the Roaring Twenties and the Great Depression, dying on the eve of America's entrance into World War II. There was a strongly evangelical quality to his disposition. It would seem that he arrived at St. Malachy's to find a languishing parish, and his zeal to serve God's people made a reinvention of the church inevitable. Theater people, he recognized, needed a church that took into account the demands of their professions. They needed his ministry. In 1920, soon after he came on board, Father Leonard turned the down-

A wide view of the Actors' Chapel as it appeared by the 1930s.

stairs chapel into the Actors' Chapel and designated it for the use of the theatrical community. He became the first spiritual director of the Catholic Actors' Guild of America, and headed out into the community, into dressing rooms and backstage.

A decade later, Father Leonard's church would still only have a few hundred regular parishioners—but attendance at its Sunday services had reached thousands. By 1930, the church was redesigned for an estimated $85,000 and subsequently rededicated. Another architect, Robert J. Reiley, was commissioned to add a wing to the west side of the structure and to renovate the rectory. The long, sloping stairs that led from the street to the main part of the church had been pushed up into the vestibule, and the organ built out under the sidewalk.

By this time, Father Leonard had become a fixture of the New York theatrical scene. He is said to have held Rudolph Valentino's hand as the actor died. Valentino's funeral mass took place at St. Malachy's and the thousands of fans who thronged the church unknowingly participated in one of the world's first modern mass-media events. Leonard's Actors' Chapel had become a dazzling space complete with a grotto of Our

A page from the marriage registry noting the union of Douglas Fairbanks, Jr., and Lucille LeSueur (aka, Joan Crawford).

Lady of Lourdes and a marble altar and altar rail donated by vaudevillian luminaries and George M. Cohan.

As one writer of the period effused:

Then, instead of turning away from Broadway, Father Leonard reached out hands and joined with it! Instead of closing the doors of St. Malachy's, he opened them wider! And now, today, St. Malachy's, the actors' church, and Father Leonard, the actors' chaplain, stand alone in church and theater history. The little gray chapel of St. Malachy's is the theatrical profession's place to praise and pray to find extended always a hand of friendship, encouragement, help and understanding.

Also by this time, Father Leonard had gotten a dispensation to celebrate a mass at 12:10 on Sunday mornings. Members of the Metropolitan opera and figures of the jazz scene mingled their voices with other parishioners. It became known as the Actors' Mass and, alternatively, the Printers' Mass (for the pressmen down the street at the *New York Times*). Later, a 4 A.M. mass would be added—after the Great Depression and the subsequent closure of so many theaters prompted the emergence of the nightclub culture whose performers worked even odder hours than their stage brethren. The 4 A.M. mass was standing-room only. The list of those who attended the late-late mass was celebrity-filled: George M. Cohan, Spencer Tracy, Perry Como, Irene Dunne, Hildegarde, Florence Henderson, Danny Thomas, Bob Hope and Ricardo Montalban. Fred Allen, Don Ameche, Cyril Ritchard and Pat O'Brien served on the altar. Douglas Fairbanks, Jr., and Joan Crawford were married there.

Father Leonard, and his assistant, Father James B. O'Reilly, worked tirelessly and apparently in great harmony to further St. Malachy's mission. At the dedication of the newly renovated church in 1930, Cardinal Hayes praised Father Leonard as "a real priest of God who has labored

Lillian Gish, James Coco
and friends with Father
George Moore at the piano,
Christmas 1982.

Bud Abbott and Lou Costello knew St. Malachy's from their years on Broadway.

Spencer Tracy

Kaye Ballard

ate comedian Chris Farley, a committed Friendly
isitor, with Monsignor Michael Crimmins.

Vanessa Williams speaks at
St. Malachy's.

Mrs. Bob Hope and Ray Bolger

At the rectory of the
church, Father Moore
gathered with many
celebrities.

Chief Iron Eyes

Mrs. Bob Hope

Father Moore with Ray Bolger, the
Scarecrow from *The Wizard of Oz*.

Ted Knight, Pat O'Brien and Scott Brady

Ted Knight, Fibber McGee, Pat O'Brien and Paul Pigerni

amongst you with a wisdom and kindness and a broad sympathy that have made him beloved of all." Indeed, Father Leonard could be found after Sunday masses welcoming those returning from theatrical tours and blessing those about to depart. "The mission of St. Malachy's," the Cardinal continued, "is to bring Christ to those who seek Him here—You have erected a temple not only for the people of this district but also for the stranger who finds himself in this city, perhaps alone and unknown. You are here to welcome, to advise him and to help him."

Around this time Father Leonard attended a gala held at one of Broadway's largest theaters. A fifteen-act program was prepared by some of the biggest names of the day in honor of his return from a trip to Rome. The performance was followed by the presentation of a four-figure check and the applause of more than one thousand men and women gathered for the event. The priest's eyes filled with tears. "My dear flock—my dear children—have come home," he said.

Father (later, Monsignor) Leonard, served for another ten years until his death. Monsignor O'Reilly, who

Father Leonard with two young parishioners after Palm Sunday mass in 1924.

Florence Henderson

Dear Fr. Kelly—

It's very hard for me to put into words what it meant to me. Malachy's was "my church" + my place to go + regain my strength, my confidence + my soul. It was where I first took my children to Mass — when I would go often between matinee + Evening performances + when I would meet my fellow actors.

I could never imagine Broadway without St. Malachy's. They are inseparable! I am with you all in spirit + my spirit will always be a part of St. Malachy's!

God Bless + love,
Florence Henderson

had been at the church since 1926, became pastor in 1940. He served with similar zeal for the next twenty years, continuing his predecessor's involvement with the Catholic Actors' Guild of America. A vivid sense of the ministry can be gained from an interview given by Monsignor O'Reilly to a newspaper in 1943. His observations:

Actors' sins are publicized more. Show people have the reputation for being less decent. It is not true. Human nature is the same all over. . . . Actors can make their prayers and then go home to get a well-deserved rest. Otherwise, they would have to get up early with only a few hours' sleep. . . . Show people always come before an opening and pray for success. Al Jolson never failed to send a young Catholic girl to light a candle before the Grotto before he opened.

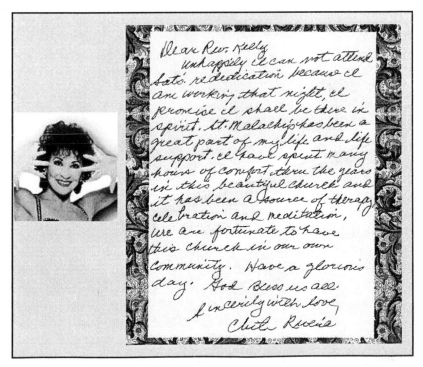

His most moving statement refers to those he helped:

Like the once prosperous vaudevillian actor, who made $500 to $750 a week, but who now hasn't room rent—we try to make him understand times have changed and we leave a few dollars when we depart. And the young girl who came to New York from a small town positive she would find fame on the stage, only she did not get a job and then became ill. . . . And the chorus girl who learns that to be 26 is to be old, and unless she has exceptional talent or a specialty number she must make way for some 18-year-old girl, but they will keep coming because the prize is great.

Monsignor O'Reilly and his assistants, like Father Leonard before him, regularly visited every theater dressing room, nightclub and hotel, because "the strength and value of the church to them is to keep them close to God. It gives them the opportunity of staying decent, which means staying sane."

Although the 4 A.M. mass continued to draw a crowd, over time the crowd diminished as nightclubs closed and later acts were canceled. Monsignor O'Reilly remained

52

heavily involved with the theatrical community, as evidenced by a letter that acknowledges his successful petition to have a medal of St. Genesius made in 1947. The patron saint of actors, Genesius had been an ancient Roman comedian who mocked Christians, but found himself converted mid-act, and was martyred because of his refusal to ridicule his newfound faith.

In 1957, a letter to then Cardinal Spellman reveals a priest zealously protecting attendance at his early-morning mass times. Already, St. Malachy's 4 A.M. mass had seen attendance drop precipitously after a neighboring church had introduced a mass at the same time. Now the Monsignor was faced with similar competition for

Painting of St. Genesius, the patron saint of actors, that once hung in the lower chapel.

the 12:10 A.M. mass, and he wrote: "I can assure Your Eminence there is as much need for this mass as there is for a fur coat in New York during the month of July." His request that the new mass be denied was turned down. Three years later on March 20, 1960, after two decades as pastor and thirty-four years of total service to St. Malachy's, Monsignor O'Reilly died after a walk around the neighborhood.

The details of the next eighteen years are sparse. Two priests, Monsignors Phillip J. Nolan and Thomas J. O'Brien served between 1960 and 1978. What *is* clear is that they presided over the decline of the neighborhood and the related decline of St. Malachy's. Although average monthly attendance on Sundays was a robust 16,000 in 1969, by 1978 the parish and its immediate surroundings were embattled. Pornographers and prostitutes had overrun the area, the basement Actors' Chapel had long been closed.

It was during this time that Monsignor George Moore, ensconced in a comfortable parish in Riverdale, was given a mandate by then Cardinal Cooke: "Make it work, or the Archdiocese will have to close it down." The Cardinal had made it clear that this might be a

54

Father Moore took to the streets to help reclaim St. Malachy's neighborhood.

Father Moore standing in front of one symptom of urban decline in
the late 1970s.

"I was an actor, and St. Malachy's was always there."
—Edward Hermann, actor

thankless and grueling task. Moore, an ebullient man barely able to contain his many ideas, embraced the job.

In a 1976 letter to the chancery, he wonders: "How to witness Christ in Times Square? How to help His Eminence and the Archdiocese realize a commitment to an image of St. Malachy's as a vibrant, viable Catholic voice speaking to and for the people of God in this great city?" But he was resolved: "There are problems here, but the important thing is to keep trying. Sometimes you fall on your face, but you get up again. You simply can't give up the fight." Although it looked like closure was imminent, Moore fought.

"I spent the first three years walking the streets exploring the turf. I talked to everybody—cops, hookers, short-order cooks, everybody. There are lots of beautiful people here," Moore would later recall. He predicted that a portion of Eighth Avenue, known as the "Minnesota Strip" for its proliferation of young prostitutes and runaways from the Midwest, would be so changed by the positive community efforts he helped bring about that its moniker

 *Philip J. Smith is the president of the Shubert Organization, the largest theater owner on Broadway. He started his career selling tickets at the box office in the 1950s. Back then a night's work at the theater ended with a midnight show: eight acts of vaudeville for seventy-five minutes and a film lasting seventy-five to ninety minutes. Afterward, many headed to St. Malachy's for mass at 4 A.M.*

Mr. Smith remembers how safe the area was during that heady time—he had no qualms about his fiancée traveling on the subway to Times Square for the New Year's Eve celebration. It was as part of the effort to restore the area to this level of safety (after the decline of the 1960s and 1970s) that Mr. Smith recalls St. Malachy's really charging ahead "to restore the standard of life in the community."

> *"Our best Christmas happened during the [renovation] construction period. The parish manager piled bales of hay on the scaffolding, which was all over the church, and then put the crèche in it. It was the most authentic-looking Nativity scene we ever had."*
>
> —*Gloria Ross*, longtime parishioner

would be forgotten. (Have *you* ever heard the term?) He worked in close association with the Mayor's Midtown Citizens' Committee, still chaired today by Gerald Schoenfeld of the Shubert Organization and Community Board 5, where he served as chairman for a time. It is easy to forget, given the present strength of the theater district, just how terrible things were then and how the idea of renewal seemed almost absurd.

Words written at the dedication of Encore, the parish's now immensely successful senior citizen program (the brainchild of Moore, who recognized that his area had the highest concentration of seniors in Manhattan), serve as a powerful reminder:

Sleazy bars, pornographic enterprises of all kinds, transient "hotels" of dubious distinction abound.

59

Criminals, prostitutes, drug pushers have built a multimillion-dollar trade. Local police, welfare agencies and people and merchants of good will are fighting what sometimes seems like only a holding action against total corruption.

It was almost as if the recently concluded conflict in Vietnam had found its way to Times Square under the name "urban decay." But according to Moore, St. Malachy's wouldn't just hold, it would act to change its surroundings:

St. Malachy's, under a loving mandate from Cardinal Cooke refuses to fold before the squalid tide that has moved over Broadway and midtown. St. Malachy's stands in defiance of decay. St. Malachy's has resolved to act—not simply as a church, but as a force for the good of all who live and work where we live and work.

Cesar Romero   Oct. 19, 1993

Dear Rev. Kelly:
My congratulations and best wishes to you and
St. Malachy's for everything that you do to
serve the theatrical community of New York.
Sincerely,
Cesar Romero

Indeed, these words, appearing as they did on November 1, 1977, marked a turning point in the battle for St. Malachy's and its neighborhood. Father Moore informed Cardinal Cooke that he would sell the marble altar and rail from the Actors' Chapel to help stretch St. Malachy's limited resources. The basement of the church was converted into a senior center and dedicated by Cardinal Cooke as an outpost "in defiance of decay."

A year later, on November 19, 1978, Father Moore dedicated a carillon that would chime every quarter-hour and mark evening and matinee show times with "There's No Business Like Show Business." The $9,000 needed for the bells had come from theatrical and business neighbors. Throughout its history, and especially in this hour of need, people of many faiths gathered around St. Malachy's to support their church. "Church bells, ringing out above all this

61

we see around us, will be a reassurance to the many wonderful people here while telling the purveyors of slime and sleaze, 'There's something else here besides you.'"

In addition to cultivating strong relationships with local businesses and theater organizations, Father Moore rented out the basement as a performance space to theater groups. He had a deep love of theater:

Because the rest of us have our problems and pressures, one of the greatest things these people do for us is to transport us out of all that. At the same time, through acting, music or the written word, what is very frequently realized is another aspect of the beauty of God.

Once again, St. Malachy's began to see its status as the Actors' Chapel renewed. Father Moore's photogenic face appears in article after article recounting the grand history of the church and the priest's heroic work.

Upon Father Moore's death in 1990 (his funeral was a standing-room-only event attended by the mayor), Father Michael C. Crimmins became the pastor of St. Malachy's.

The 1990s witnessed a revitalization of the area and the realization of many of Father Moore's dreams. Father Crimmins and Father Joseph Kelly, the parochial vicar,

Father Moore standing in front of the Eugene O'Neill theater in the late 1970s.

St. Malachy's mid-century.

worked well together and capitalized on the emerging opportunities to invigorate St. Malachy's further. Businesses and residents streamed in and new construction was everywhere. A sale of air rights above the church arranged by Father Crimmins generated the funds needed to finally restore the church. St. Malachy's received a new roof, the cleaning of its exterior, and the renovation of the interior during which the pews were angled and the heating and air-conditioning systems updated.

Monsignor Crimmins and Father Joseph Kelly continued the tradition of a church that celebrates the neighborhood and the larger theatrical community in which St. Malachy's exists. Father Erno, who followed Monsignor Crimmins, oversaw the arrival of the church's centennial and the renaming of the street outside to "St. Malachy's Way," as it looked forward to the next hundred years. And Father Richard Baker seems intent on renewing St. Malachy's commitment to Broadway and the next generation in the life of this church.

ALL THAT I HAVE WRITTEN here is at best just a sketch of the very long and profound life of a church. This book aspires through photographs, articles and the recollections of many individuals to illuminate St. Malachy's.

The writers, photographers and recorders of this book are all volunteers and I thank them heartily for their efforts. But failure is inevitable in such an aspiration. Nothing can capture the vibrancy, diversity and stunning breadth of one hundred years in the life of this church.

Part of my encounter with St. Malachy's has entailed listening to memories of the church that was (and is). Bob Cunningham, a devoted parishioner of St. Malachy's, comes to mind. Bob was an actor. He can be seen in this book astride a horse (Bob played a cowboy in many a Hollywood western). I did not know him well, but I saw him frequently at mass and one day he invited me to the theater. I accepted.

Bob Cunningham, parishioner, astride a horse in one of his many westerns.

Afterwards, we walked through Times Square. He was eighty-something at the time. He told me about the Catholic Actors' Guild of America and about Spencer Tracy and George M. Cohan, and so many different actors that I could not remember all their names. It seemed such a vibrant world of people of common profession, of common faith, uniting around a place they all shared in common, St. Malachy's—a sacred place that was theirs. For a moment, standing in the Times Square of 2001, I had the curious feeling that another, older world was about to emerge, burst through the towers and neon of the present like an actor tumbling through a paper scrim. I always meant to speak with Bob again, but my schedule changed and I didn't see him as often. He died in 2002 and with his death that older world grew a bit more elusive and out of reach.

So the end is finally reached. I hope that the journey has been entertaining and illuminating, but not enough to satisfy. Certainly not the main course, not even the appetizer—an invitation with a compelling notion of a place and a spirit yet to be discovered would be good enough.

The people are still in the pews here at St. Malachy's, the young and the old. Speak especially to the old. You will find them at 12:15 mass on the weekdays (the nocturnal service discontinued long ago) or downstairs at Encore for breakfast or lunch. Some are homebound now. So many stories: chorus girls who remember the 4 A.M., parishioners who recall with furtive glee the time a con artist posed as a priest, and vivid memories of the giants of stage and screen serving at the altar or flitting between the columns to light a candle or kneel to pray before a show.

Rather than speak about himself for this book, Monsignor Crimmins characteristically directed attention to someone else—Virginia Barrows—when he chose to recall his memories. She had been one of St. Malachy's most committed and energetic parishioners. Even near the end of her life, when she became very ill, she stayed involved, kept volunteering and encouraged others to keep St. Malachy's community strong. A holy and loveable presence, he called her, and a reservoir of the church's history while she lived. Monsignor Crimmins knew that the strength of St. Malachy's resides in its cast: the cameo-makers and the leads.

So don't hesitate. Day after day, the eyes of the last century are closing and if St. Malachy's second century is to prove worthwhile, it will be because what those eyes have seen has been passed down.

Detail from the mosaic of the Sacred Heart in
St. Malachy's West Chapel.

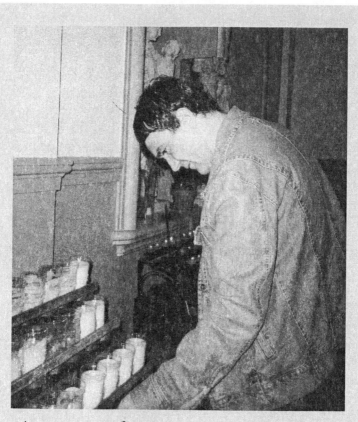

Antonio Banderas *sits in a cozy dressing room in the Eugene O'Neill Theater. He graciously fetches chairs for his visitors. It is only an hour before he has to be on stage and only a week before he will leave* Nine, *a stage adaptation of Fellini's 8-1/2.* Nine *is this prodigious screen actor's first show on Broadway.*

"I discovered St. Malachy's in 1984," Banderas

says. It was his first time in America, when he traveled under the auspices of the Spanish Institute of Cinematography, which was trying to promote Spanish movies in New York. Banderas took the opportunity to plunge into the theater district.

"I was in love with musicals for a long time, so I came to Broadway to see two musicals. One of them was a Bob Fosse musical called The Big Deal. It was a flop. The critics killed [it]. . . . But I loved it. I loved it. That set up my relationship with critics. . . .

"I saw Bernadette Peters playing in a musical called Song and Dance. And then, I just walked. I walked on Broadway. I went to every store that I could to buy a shirt or a hat or some musical sheets, and then I found this church, the Actors' Chapel."

He entered the church and after sitting for a while in one of the pews, a priest approached him. The priest told him that he, too, was from Spain, as he related St. Malachy's history and its involvement with actors.

"I can remember just sitting down in the church and saying, 'Jesus, I would love to work in this place [Broadway] someday.'"

Banderas smiles wistfully and continues, "It was twenty years ago. . . . Jesus took a long time."

The intervening twenty years saw Banderas ascend to the top of his profession, but the desire "to work in this place" went unfulfilled until Nine. When he arrived in New York to begin work at the play, he returned to St. Malachy's.

"I've been going there very often. Especially at the beginning, when I didn't know what was going to happen. I used to go there—it is a traditional thing to do this once a week—and light nine candles. I did it the day of the opening. I did it the day that we opened on reviews. And I have been going there . . . at the beginning, just asking for things . . . but lately, I've been going just to think. . . ."

It was a dream to have reached Broadway. "Hollywood was not my target," Banderas muses. "Hollywood happened as an accident almost."

Broadway delivered on its twenty-year-old promise and Banderas was sad to leave. He says he will never forget St. Malachy's, to which he has turned, as have generations of actors before him, to pray for things that actors need.

"I ask for help . . . for lucidity and to have the capacity of overcoming fear," he says. "It is a constant in our profession."

Antonio Banderas in his dressing room for *Nine*.

ST. MALACHY'S NEIGHBORHOOD

Mary Brendle, Community District 4 Historian

[Clinton and Chelsea]

JOHN BARRYMORE, of the legendary theatrical family, debuted on the New York
stage in 1903, the same year the
Archdiocese of New York established St.
Malachy's parish.

Both events occurred in a vibrant
community called Clinton, perhaps
better known by its sobriquet "Hell's
Kitchen." The district boundaries ran
from Fifth Avenue to the Hudson,
between 34th and 59th Streets. In the
1960s, commercial development and
city delineation moved the eastern line

The west side of Broadway between 47th and 50th streets, 1909.

to Eighth Avenue, but St. Malachy's remains an integral part of a neighborhood whose roots run deep.

When Broadway officially opened in 1703 as Bloemendaal Road, farmland covered most of the area. The road went north from New Amsterdam—at the tip of the island—to Albany, with farm lanes branching off to the villages of Greenwich, Bloomingdale, Harsenville and Harlem. In Bloomingdale in 1714, Mathew Hopper reclaimed a large portion of the land grant given to his father, Andries, in 1652, and built his homestead at what would become 50th Street and Broadway. His son John the Elder, born in 1706, inherited the farm and built homes for two of his sons. The third, Andrew, remained at home until his death in 1821 at 85 years of age. As city growth moved northward, buildings began lining streets laid out on paper in a grid system in 1811. Land speculator William Vanderbilt bought Andrew's property to sell in lot parcels.

Although the area was still part of Bloomingdale, in the late-eighteenth century George Clinton, first governor of the New York territory, acquired property on Manhattan's west side. His nephews DeWitt and George Clinton Jr. married children of area landowners, as did several of his nieces. In 1839 a Clinton horsecar line ran from West 48th Street to 20th Street, where passengers could connect with a carriage to Canal Street. Supposedly, the governor's land included a still-standing, renovated coach house on West 46th Street. The Clinton presence could well have given the neighborhood its name.

A line of newly built theater-district row houses circa 1900.

The opening of the Erie Canal in 1825 spurred growth of industries along the North River shore and the construction of small wooden houses to accommodate immigrants in search of work. The city claimed farmland lots to build Eighth, Ninth, Tenth and Eleventh Avenues, and 39th through 48th Streets. Private brick homes and tenements began replacing shanties. An enormous exhibition hall called the Crystal Palace went up on the site of the former Croton water distribution center between 40th and 42nd Streets, from Fifth to Sixth Avenues. Crowds visited from 1853 to 1858 when fire destroyed the entire structure within minutes. Miraculously, two thousand people fled the building and there were no deaths. The public research library and Bryant Park now fill the two blocks.

Close to the river, coal, wagon and builder yards, two breweries, other industries and tenements intermixed. During the last quarter of the century, immigrants from Ireland arrived in large numbers and settled primarily between Eighth and Tenth Avenues. Around the turn of the century a substantial Italian population joined them. Others arrived from Greece, Germany, Poland; racial diversity became a characteristic of the neighborhood. Many of the populace endured crowded, unsanitary,

> *"Lots of movie stars took up the collection, people like Don Ameche and Jimmy Durante. They would blend in with the crowd that attended the mass—they did not stand out because they did not want to stand out."*
>
> —Cathy Anzalone, longtime parishioner

impoverished conditions. According to a *New York Times* article of 1881, crime dominated 38th and 39th Streets between Ninth and Tenth Avenues. A building called "Hell's Kitchen" stood there; the Hell's Kitchen Gang roamed the streets. This could well explain why the name soon identified those blocks and gradually the whole area, despite the neighborhood's great majority of law-abiding folks.

Along with the northward population push, the city's entertainment center moved from downtown to the 14th Street area, then to 23rd and finally the West 40s, gradually replacing the carriage industry surrounding Longacre Square at 42nd Street. The American Theater, the first on 42nd, preceded eighty theaters built by the turn of the century. The Metropolitan Concert Hall arrived on 41st at Broadway in 1880. Poor attendance

Daytime street scene in the theater district circa 1910.

recycled it into the Casino Roller Skating Rink and Exhibition Hall, and finally led to its demolition in 1887.

At Broadway and 44th Street the Olympia Music Hall offered opera, ballet, vaudeville and a concert promenade all at the same time. Tenements sprinkled through

The neighborhood around St. Malachy's in its first decade.

the blocks east of Eighth Avenue as residential growth continued primarily to its west. The 1855 Methodist-Episcopal Asylum for the Aged and Infirm on West 42nd Street was converted to the Clinton Apartment House in 1883. Hartley House, one of the oldest settlement houses in the city, opened on West 46th Street in 1897 to serve the needy.

When St. Malachy's opened at 243 West 49th, three-story brick residential buildings lined 49th Street in an area of mixed uses. Pastor William J. B. Daly lived in 239; Number 247 housed a sanitarium. A smokehouse operated at 209-11; Theodore Grunewald sold shoes from 200 and walked to work from his home at 155 West 51st Street. The Metropolitan Railway Company horse-car stables filled half the block between 49th and 50th Streets west of Eighth Avenue; the American Horse Exchange lay at Broadway and 50th Street, now the site of the Wintergarden Theater. The Old Guard Armory sat

> *"Even when I lived far away, I would make mass at St. Malachy's."*
>
> —*Bob Grogan*, longtime parishioner

at the east corner of 49th and Broadway; automobile showrooms proliferated, but residents continued to fill tenements. St. Malachy's based a parish club for young men in Washington Hall at 781 Eighth Avenue in 1920. Just up the avenue lived a dancer girlfriend of speakeasy owner "Legs Diamond." During the 1927–8 season, 257

Cardinal Hayes and Father Leonard lead the procession during the rededication of St Malachy's in 1930.

Commercial buildings abounded in the area surrounding St. Malachy's.

plays opened in 71 theaters within the district. St. Malachy's geared services to unique work schedules.

Commercialization steadily pushed residents to Eighth Avenue and the west. By 1950 Clinton's population totaled over 62,000: approximately two-thirds native white, one quarter foreign-born white, close to 5 percent Puerto Rican, close to 5 percent African American, and

"I will not have another church until I die."
—*Thelma Walsh*, longtime parishioner

A bustling theater district at the turn of the century.

a small portion of others. Within the next five years the Puerto Rican numbers more than doubled. A 1969 study found about 85 percent of the residents living east of Tenth Avenue, with the balance in tenements to its west amid auto-body-repair shops, factories, warehouses, parking lots and garages. This remains largely accurate today, although media-related firms and artists form a significant group

The 1970s triggered the creation of a number of not-for-profit organizations designed to address special needs. Project Find came in 1971 to serve seniors. The Ninth Avenue Business Association launched a festival in 1973 to draw attention to the wide variety of ethnic restaurants and food shops along the avenue; thousands of people continue to attend its annual weekend celebration. Father George Moore, St. Malachy's pastor in 1977, brought Dominican nuns Sister Elizabeth Hasselt and Sister Lillian McNamara to St. Malachy's to serve needy elderly persons in Clinton and Times Square. He moved the Actors' Chapel into the church; Encore Community Services opened in the lower-level space, offering meals and other social services. A decade later the organization acquired the Hotel

Markwell (where Jack Benny once lived) to offer housing and on-site supportive services to formerly homeless elderly persons in the renamed Encore 49, and are currently engaged in a new construction project on Tenth Avenue.

Also in the 1970s, neighborhood groups began petitioning city officials to combat rampant vice along 42nd Street and Eighth Avenue. The Clinton Planning Council, formed in 1959, and the Ninth Avenue Business Association took the lead in a vigorous fight against the proliferation of drugs, prostitution, pornographic materials and general "sleaze" along the "Deuce," as 42nd Street came to be known. Father Moore of St. Malachy's and Father Robert Rappleyea, pastor of Holy Cross Church on 42nd Street, played important roles in the effort that led to legislation eliminating "massage parlors" and creating a Midtown Enforcement city agency based within the neighborhood. This began a renewal now in evidence. At Father Moore's invitation Community Board 5 held its monthly meetings at St. Malachy's for over a decade, and he served as an active member. In his autobiography, the then president of the New York Public Library remembered waiting in a church basement until 11 P.M. to secure the Board's approval of a plan for private non-profit management of Bryant Park, a plan that has proved eminently successful.

When the neighborhood became threatened by the siting of a proposed convention center at its western edge between 43rd and 47th Streets, many voices expressed concern that development pressures could radically alter the neighborhood's character with displacement of lower- and middle-income residents, small businesses and commercial tenants. Working with community leaders, the city shaped a special Clinton district zoning plan that protects existing housing stock, yet permits controlled development along Eighth Avenue and 42nd Street. This has proved a bulwark of preservation for the community's low-scale buildings, particularly important after the city adopted a zoning change that directed commercial development away from the East Side, west of Sixth Avenue.

Presently, the neighborhood is in the throes of significant change. A *New York Times* restaurant critic in 2001 lamented that "trendy urbanites are now rushing into Hell's Kitchen to live, to work, and, yes, to eat." But, the changes are not as radical as might be expected. Newcomers seem as determined as generations-old residents to preserve a unique atmosphere. Although Clinton is repeatedly under siege because of its adjacence to the midtown commercial center, strenuous activism remains vigilant against the assault. Change and growth are absorbed without smothering a singular identity manifested in involvement with family, church, neighborliness and service.

Gerald Schoenfeld *is the Chairman of the Board of the Shubert Organization. Shubert is one of the best-known owner/operators of live-performance theaters in the United States. The organization's roots go back to the turn of the century and the emergence of Broadway as we know it today, facilitating the production of countless classic plays and musicals.*

Mr. Schoenfeld played a special role both in the history of the Shubert Organization and the major renaissance that reclaimed Broadway for theatergoers and residents alike. He revitalized Shubert and during his tenure brought dozens of now-famous productions to the stage, among them: Amadeus, An Inspector Calls, The Life and Adventures of Nicholas Nickleby, The Most Happy Fella, Children of a Lesser God, The Heidi Chronicles, Little Shop of Horrors, *and* Cats.

But his greatest legacy is likely to be what he has done (and continues to do) for Times Square and its surroundings. It is this legacy and the story behind it that unites Schoenfeld's vision and action to St. Malachy's, the Actors' Chapel.

Schoenfeld recently sat down to chat about a

chapter in his life when he witnessed New Yorkers joining together to take on urban decline, and refusing to lose their city to it.

The decline of Times Square began in the 1960s and accelerated at an incredible pace, turning the theater district into a perilous and forbidding place filled with X-rated theaters, drugs and prostitutes (at times up to twenty-five strolled per block). Schoenfeld remembers walking down the street one day with his wife and lamenting the presence of piles of trash and the prostitutes. "Do something about it," his wife suggested, and Schoenfeld did.

The story of what Schoenfeld did really begins when he was appointed chairman of the Mayor's Midtown Citizens Committee in 1976.

Schoenfeld knew that action had to be taken. The decline jeopardized Shubert's business interests by impacting theater attendance, but, even more, it was heartbreaking to see the vibrancy of Broadway dimmed and its potential to be a cultural hub squandered. Unfortunately, the battle would be uphill. Even more formidable than the actual decline, Schoenfeld recalls, was the dark, defeatist attitude of so many New Yorkers. There was an acceptance of urban decay as a fact of life. When people heard about what Schoenfeld wanted to do, he was told he was wasting his time.

Schoenfeld knew he needed allies in the fight. His relationship with St. Malachy's began at this bleak point. The decline of Times Square was strangling the life out of the small church with the big theatrical pedigree.

Enter Father George Moore, stage right. Moore and Schoenfeld shared a deep commitment to turning the neighborhood around.

"There was no pretense about George," Schoenfeld remembers. The priest was larger-than-life and his outsized personality made him "a very recognizable figure in the community." Father Moore and St. Malachy's were joined by Father Robert Rappleyea and Holy Cross. Schoenfeld saw the two priests, who became fast friends, as the north and south anchors of the revitalization.

"In my mind they were the embodiment of what a priest should be. . . ."

The men formed an alliance with others in the community that continues today. Together they resisted the scoffers and refused the alternative of losing the area. Small victories and signs of positive resistance followed. Hotlines to the police stations were set up to foster better response times to crime. A hotline to City Hall followed. The police put up barricades on the sidewalks to impede the prostitution trade. Father Moore was instrumental in shutting down the Pussy Cat Theater. Schoenfeld remembers that moment as a turning point, "We all met outside the theater the day the sign came down."

Father Moore installed the carillon bells to broadcast what he called a different presence to the neighborhood—a new, positive force taking hold. And take hold it slowly did. As Schoenfeld recalls, eventually the scoffers became converts.

Then Father Moore became ill. "When George took sick, the league gave him an honorary Tony," Schoenfeld tells. He and Phil Smith visited Moore in the hospital to tell him the news. Moore was elated. "You would have thought we had given him the keys to the pearly gates."

Father Moore died, but the alliance thrived; renewal was under way and its momentum was powerful. After the Pussy Cat, other similar theaters began to close; the prostitutes and the drug pushers moved out. Serious commercial and residential construction began and it continues today, cementing the legacy forged by Schoenfeld, the concerned citizens of midtown and the little church on 49th Street.

Show biz priest fights for his floc

MEL JUFFE

The Rev. George W. Moore has his eye on a portable grand piano for a concert grand piano. He's also on the lookout

for a concert grand piano. Book store and piano are the next two major objectives in the stubborn campaign being waged by Moore, pastor of St. Malachy's Catholic Church

on W. 49th St., the long-time home of the famed Actors' Chapel, to develop his ministry in the theater district.

The book store figures in Moore's dream of creating a St. Malachy's "Green Room," where young actors

Fairbanks Jr., for example) and funerals (most notably, Rudolf Valentino) and odd-hour masses.

But as show biz went, so went its church. By the time Moore was sent in 1976 to rescue what he calls "the most unusual parish in the U.S.," attendance had dipped from 16,000 a month to a low of 8000 (a figure which has now doubled) and the church was burdened with $60,000 worth of unpaid bills.

In his first three months at St. Malachy's, he spent most of his days and nights walking through the sleaze and glitter of the streets of

his Times Square parish to assess the dimensions of the problems his church faced.

The most pressing need in the area, Moore saw, was that of the elderly poor.

Gritting his teeth, Moore removed the little-used Actors' Chapel from the church basement — selling off such sentimental treasures as the altar, donated by George M. Cohan, where Fred Allen married Portland Hoffa. The basement now houses the church's "Encore" program, which furnishes the elderly poor — about half of them Jewish and many of them for-

mer show biz people with food and comp

With "Encore" smoothly, Moore troupe of priests as began turning their tion to the new gen of Broadway enter Last November the dedicated a carillo matinees and salutes curtain-time nearby theaters "There's No Bushe Show Business."

"This is a show ish," says Moore, bells ring out to purveyors of slim sleaze, "There's sor else here besides you

JAMESBRADY

The priest of Broadway

Tom Leahy of CBS brought me this idea for a movie.

It's got everything but Barry Fitzgerald and Bing Crosby, a score by Jimmy Van Heusen and Johnny Burke, and a Mark Hellinger or Damon Runyon script.

It's the true story of a big city church, a couple of hundred old folks, real estate magnates, a bordello, two nuns, George M. Cohan, the stagehands' union, an X-rated joint called the Pussycat Theatre, an electronic carillon programmed to sound "The Angelus" but which more often played "There's No Business Like Show Business," and a priest named George Moore.

Father Moore died earlier this month of prostate cancer at age 64 and a couple of days later was nominated for a Tony Award to be given posthumously this coming Sunday. Almost everyone else in the story (except Mr. Cohan) is still alive including a star-studded cast of what those who knew George Moore call "every Jew on Broadway."

I began working on the tiny, a couple of days before Father Moore's death, on West 49th Street off Broadway, a few steps from what the music business used to call Tin Pan Alley, at a little old Catholic church called St. Malachy's, a New York landmark known as "the Actors' Chapel."

Fred Allen was married there, Don Ameche and Pat O'Brien served as altar boys, Cohan donated the marble altar, and it was where Spencer Tracy and Irene Dunne and Bob Hope heard mass.

But in 1976 Archbishop Cooke decided to close down the old church, reduced to a home for aging priests. Madison Square Garden had

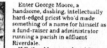

Brady

Enter George Moore, a handsome, dashing, intellectually hard-edged priest who'd made something of a name for himself as a fund-raiser and administrator running a parish in affluent Riverdale.

If Father Moore analyzed St. Malachy's and concluded it wasn't worth saving, the Archdiocese would close it down. As Fr. Moore walked the streets he found this was no longer a Broadway neighborhood, no gathering of actors, but the highest density area of single-room-occupancy hotels in town. On the block with St. Malachy's were the Pussycat Theatre with its show shows and the most successful male bordello in Manhattan. Then there were the pimps and the dealers and the muggers and the hookers and, you name it. And there were the elderly poor, to whom no one was ministering.

The church itself is on the ground floor, a beautiful jewel box of a place. Downstairs, another chapel, a big one. Fr. Moore went to work. Why not open up the space and create a senior citizens' center?

But he needed help. Fr. Moore phoned around to various nuns, asking for volunteers. Sister Lillian McNamara, a Dominican with a Master of Fine Arts in music, was the first to respond. Shortly after, a more delicate-appearing soul, Sister Elizabeth Hasselt, arrived.

"George was the gusto," Sister Lillian told me, "Elizabeth was the brains and I was semi-brawn." They found a handyman who went to work tearing the basement apart. "He unbolted the pews and we broke up the marble altar and the local grammar

Priestly Roles

The Rev. John McCullagh bids farewell to Mother Teresa as she leaves St. Malachy's Church. Its pastor, the Rev. George Moore, looks on.

JOHN PEDIN DAILY NEWS

Saint's presence warms cit

6/5/81

Mother Teresa hears Mass he

By MARCIA KRAMER

Mother Teresa made New York City her own today, carrying a message of peace and love—a love that she said should extend to all, especially unborn children.

The tiny, frail-looking nun from Calcutta continued her crusade against abortion, saying that the unborn child should be protected because he "is created in God's image."

"Let us pray that no mother, no wife, no woman

Bill Reel talks to Mother Teresa. Page 6.

will forget her role and destroy the fruit of her womb—the unborn child," she said during a speech before about 500 members of the Regina Coeli society of the New York City Police Department. "If you know anyone who doesn't want the child, who is afraid of the child, then tell them to give that child to me," she continued in a barely audible whisper.

Mother Teresa, who won the Nobel Peace Prize for her work among India's poor, started her day by participating in a Mass for Regina Coeli members at St. Malachy's Church at 239 W. 49th St., the show business church in the theater district.

She did what she does best—serve. During the offertory procession, Mother Teresa carried the

sacramental wine to the altar for the celeb Rev. John McCullagh, a Police Department from Brooklyn.

Clutching a worn set of rosary beads in hand and wearing brown sandals and a he woolen sweater over her blue-trimmed wh despite the 75-degree heat, Mother Teresa, w was escorted into the church by St. Malachy the Rev. George Moore. He said later that he had an opportunity to talk with her. "But is to touch a saint?" he said.

"She's a great woman," agreed Dolly G one of the worshipers. "She works for should build a monument to her here."

The small church was filled with the wom the Regina Coeli, who had invited the famo address its annual breakfast later in the m the Sheraton Centre hotel.

Mother Teresa brought Christ's simple me "Love one another"—to the city last night, w stopped in at Covenant House, the Re Ritter's home for abandoned and abused chi teenage runaways.

She praised Ritter's "beautiful work" and as the center's youngsters serenaded h presented her an "I love New York" butt T-shirt bearing the Covenant House "U symbol.

A HALF BLOCK OFF BROADWAY, FATHER GEORGE MOORE OVERSEES THE MIRACLE OF 49TH STREET

next time you're waiting in a box line at a Broadway theater and ar *There's No Business Like Business* chiming up and down eets off Times Square, you're lucinating. It's the bells of St. Ma-s reminding everyone that, in the of the pastor, Father George ore, "God is in residence on West reet, too."

years ago, when Father Moore ked to leave his middle-income Catholic parish in Riverdale, take over the 73-year-old Ac-hapel, St. Malachy's had all en up its struggle to survive the derelicts, porno impresarios ostitutes. "It was awful! The ll never rang; the phone never Moore recalls. "Oh, you got your onal drifter coming by for a t, but it was like living in a tomb. e had $60,000 worth of unpaid wondered what I had gotten my-o."

Moore, 54, also knew that St. Ma-s had for years served as the parish for show business folks y capacity—from dressers, ands and usherettes to Broad-ers, including Spencer Tracy, pe, Don Ameche, Ricardo Mon-Irene Dunne and Perry Como. lien, Jimmy Durante and Dom e had been married there.

h Valentino's massive funeral en conducted from the altar. re began a three-month walking the area, "talking to anybody uld listen," to get to know the and their problems. "This e no other parish I had ever of," he says. "We had one argest concentrations of el-oor in Manhattan. The theater had to be revived. We had nds of business people who nto the area every day, and on

rs come here for counseling," says Fa-Moore. "They ask us to marry them, bury them and 'say a prayer for us, please.'"

Photographs by Jack Vartoogian

Rudolph Valentino was buried from St. Ma-lachy's Actors Chapel in 1926. Among the pallbearers was Douglas Fairbanks Sr.

weekends the tourists. It was a craz bag."

Moore set about tackling the prob lems in often unorthodox ways. He applied for and received federal go ernment grants to set up a senior citizens' center and provide hot lun es. To make room, he closed off an renovated the seldom-used lower chapel, sold off its pews and conver ed a religious shrine into an Astro-Turfed underground garden alive w

re, who studied voice and piano ides over an impromptu lineup of :luding (from left) former chorine Ida

Davis (in the original production of *No! No! Nan-ette*), Detroit hoofer Willie Shepherd and onetime Ruffino Opera singer Mae Fortine

HELEN Hayes joins forces with Mayor Koch yesterday to deliver a little chicken — and a lot of hom — to a homebound elderly actor. Broadway trouper Larry O'Dell, 88, who receives hot lunches from City-

HAMMING IT UP – WITH CHICKE

Program during the week, set down yesterday to a chicken dinner. The meal was to attract donations to the Citymeals on Wheels, which

program leaves off. Donatio be sent to Citymeals on New York City Dept. for the 280 Broadway, Room 21

New York Post/Marc V

ENCORE:
A BEACON OF HOPE
FOR SENIORS
ON BROADWAY

Writer Mary Higgins Clark with Sister Elizabeth Hasselt.

BROADWAY'S LONGEST RUNNING show does not have elaborate costumes or a dazzling multimillion-dollar set. Its marquee is not trimmed with bright lights and bold letters listing its star performers. Huge posters with glowing media reviews do not adorn the exterior of its building. Limousines and taxis do not jostle for position curbside at its entrance. Except for a large banner decorated with shades of yellow, purple and blue and a small distinctive red heart, it is easy to walk past the Encore Center. If you do, you are missing the theater district's most important act.

Sister Lillian McNamara with Duffy, Encore's mascot.

Located in the lower level of St. Malachy's Church, formerly the Actors' Chapel, Encore, which bills itself as "Broadway's Longest Running Act of Loving Care," is a haven of comfort for low-income elderly in the Clinton and Times Square communities. Founded in 1977 by the late Reverend George Moore, pastor of St. Malachy's, Sister Elizabeth Hasselt, the center's executive director, and Sister Lillian McNamara, head of senior services, this nondenominational center began modestly, serving twenty-five meals a day. Today Encore's breakfast and lunch program feeds more than 430 people daily, delivers another 165 meals to shut-ins and provides 800 more meals on weekends.

Sister Lillian remembers the early days. "I and several seniors used to pick up our food at Horn and Hardart on 57th Street and carry it back here," she said. Conceived as a place where seniors could escape the squalor of cramped apartments in run-down tenements and dingy crime-infested, single-room occupancies, the

Sister Lillian and Elizabeth with Encore volunteers.

West 49th Street center is, instead, warm and friendly. When asked why St. Malachy's geared their ministry toward the plight of the elderly, Sister Lillian said, "Father Moore pounded the pavement. He touched base with block associations, community groups, churches and discovered many elderly living in substandard conditions, lacking support."

Encore is more than a place to chat and eat. It is filled with friends, neighbors and caring professionals.

Sisters Lillian and Elizabeth with some of the Encore staff in the kitchen.

Social workers, a part-time nurse and scores of volunteers treat the seniors with respect and dignity. Sidney Friedman, a retired postal clerk and a nine-year resident of the Encore 49 Residence, who stayed at the Bellevue Men's Shelter shortly before moving here, said "I like this place very much. It is safe, very comfy, very proper." Once a trained concert pianist who studied at Juilliard, he added, "And I get to practice my music. We have a piano here and at the center. I play Broadway show tunes and popular hits at all the parties."

Encore provides support services for homebound seniors or shut-ins to enable them to live independently. Forced to remain at home due to fragile health, often impoverished, without family or friends nearby, these forgotten seniors cannot shop, cook, clean or tend to their medical needs alone. The Friendly Visiting Program matches volunteers, often younger professionals, with seniors. Volunteers are asked to visit their "senior" friend weekly—to talk, go for walks or read to those with failing eyesight. Tied in with this are Meals-on-Wheels, the Shop and Escort Service, and Telephone Assurance Program where callers check in on the elderly twice a week.

Encore has expanded substantially since it first

opened twenty-five years ago. It administers an array of programs, social events and services to over 14,000 seniors annually. Encore offers weekly classes in painting and crafts. Seniors take yoga, shiatsu, tai chi and aerobics. There are dances, birthday and holiday celebrations, movies and concerts. Encore has a strong rapport with the Shubert Organization and the theater community, so seniors receive free tickets to Broadway and off-Broadway shows.

Its full-time, on-site,certified social workers provide one-on-one benefits and entitlement counseling. They help with Medicare, Medicaid, housing, and financial and legal matters such as living wills. There are crisis intervention and mental health services, including the Bridge Project, which lends comfort through its bereavement and grief support.

Long an advocate for decent and affordable housing for seniors, Encore opened a single-room-occupancy-style home in 1989 in the Markwell Hotel on West 49th Street. Home to 89 formerly homeless seniors with special needs, this safe, well-maintained facility provides an array of support services that have helped residents move from life on the streets and in shelters to home living.

"There is a desperate need for decent and affordable

housing for senior and low-income families in our area," Sister Lillian said. "Seniors live on fixed incomes. They cannot afford exorbitant rents. They cannot move. They have no options." Next on the agenda is the Encore West Residence on Tenth Avenue between 51st and 52nd Streets, an 84-unit development to provide additional housing to low-income seniors.

"Encore is a role model of how it can and should be done," Sister Lillian said. "We look at the senior as a complete human being. A person needs food, but also housing and other services. And that's our mission."

ACTING KIDS

Matthew Gumley, 9, has been performing for most of his life. At the age of three, he sang "The Star Spangled Banner" before a large crowd at a sporting event. Other appearances followed, but a little over two years ago he and his family moved to New York from Florida, when Matthew had been cast in Beauty and the Beast as Chip, the only role for a child in the Broadway show.

The family found an apartment near Broadway, and Matthew's older brother Eric, also an actor, began attending the Professional Performing Arts School in midtown Manhattan. Matthew had a rigorous performance schedule (he stayed with the show for over a year), but things began to settle into a routine. So the family started looking for a church and they found one in St. Malachy's.

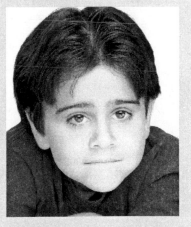

Matthew was drawn to the parish, where he was struck by the friendliness, peace, and sense of safety—a place that was soothing and welcoming. He wanted to make his first communion, but his performance schedule made it impossible for him to attend the preparatory classes. His mother, Teresa, remembers how determined Matthew was, and how he called up Father Baker to ask if anything could be done. Father Baker helped, so Matthew made his first communion and also became an altar server. Today he can usually be seen serving the 11 A.M. mass on Sunday.

His work in Beauty and the Beast *is done, but Matthew, already a member of EQUITY, SAG and AFTRA, is still working hard with recent roles in* Drake & Josh *on Nickelodeon and* The Music Man *on tour. As with generations of actors before him, St. Malachy's has become Matthew's oasis. Every time he walks by, Teresa recounts, Matthew insists that they stop in and light a candle. Her son would come to St. Malachy's every day if he could.*

ACTING KIDS

"Hey, it's the Actors' Chapel, and I'm an actor," **Jay Michael Reist,** *13, thought when he first discovered St. Malachy's. He had passed the church many times, but finally he and his family tried it out. They had recently arrived in New York to pursue Jay Michael's acting and dance ambitions.*

Beyond all the other adjustments to life in Manhattan, they craved finding a parish where they would belong. They found St. Malachy's.

Today, his mom, Louise, teaches Religious Education at the church and Jay Michael is an altar server. Since arriving in New York, his acting and dancing have blossomed. He is enrolled at the highly selective Professional Performing Arts School, recently appeared in the off-Broadway musical Dear Edwina, Jr., *and is gearing up for* Seussical Jr.

He prays at the church before shows and is well aware of St. Malachy's long relationship with actors, as well as its history, which encompasses the church's struggle through the dark period of the Minnesota Strip. That was a brief time, Jay Michael says, when St. Malachy's was "closed off"—an aberration far from most of its rich history, and quite different from the open and welcoming place that this young actor and dancer enjoys today.